To Be...
in Africa

a story told to the rhythm of an African drum.

BY DARIA BARWINSKA

Global Student Solutions
Anderson IN

To contact the author or publisher or to order additional copies of this book:

To Be... in Africa
Global Student Solutions
700 Meridian Suite 250
Anderson IN 46016
info@globalstudentweb.org

ISBN 1442163593
EAN-13 9781442163591

Cover Art by SR Martin
Editing and layout by SR Martin

CONTENTS

Thank you to the Martin family for showing me the real Kenya and giving me the full experience and caring for me.

Thank you to Emily Wasonga for simply telling me to go home with her.

Special thanks to my parents for their endless support and trust in me. I love you.

TO BE... IN AFRICA

A story told to the rhythm of an African drum.

Preface

My life journey started a long time back, in Poland with my parents. It then continued as I moved to the U.S. for University. This is just a part of it but a very important part. I describe on the following pages three weeks of my life. Those three weeks when I traveled to Kenya with a group from Anderson University. I spent my time in Kenya observing, learning and understanding the culture of the people who live there. Not only that but also understanding myself. The knowledge I gained is priceless and comes from the wisdom of locals and my own observations. I tried to live those days to the fullest, absorb as many of new things as possible, letting myself dive deep into the culture, language, cuisine, and everything that is new to me, accepting it, learning, and applying it. I also tried to give as much of myself to others as possible, sharing or just being present with them.

An old Indian saying states that to evaluate someone, you need to cross the mountains and waters that he had to cross before. It is true. That is why I decided to join those people in Kenya, in their daily lives, to understand them better. Africa, a place that is a home for so many, became hospitable to me. It's a place that is driven by a rhythm. It is a place that lives by the beat of the drum: synchronized, eternal, primordial.

Now, I close my eyes, free my mind, and remember. I remember how it is TO BE IN AFRICA…

May 8, 2007

As I wake up at 6:50 in the morning, it has not hit me yet that I am here, facing a long journey to Africa. There is no excitement or anxiety either. It just seems like another ordinary day has begun. My big green luggage standing at the door is the only thing that indicates that something is going to be different.

Breakfast, shower, e-mail my parents.

I think I am ready. I start walking down to the parking lot to meet the rest of the team going to Kenya. About fifteen minutes later, the transportation to Chicago arrives, appearing to be an unspoken indicator for everyone who is going for the trip to show up too. As the time of departure approaches, the crowd is getting bigger and bigger.

There is a freshness of the morning, with a little dew on the grass and gentle wind, which mixes with the excitement that is starting to grow. It is saturating the air around.

I leave the city of Anderson, Indiana at 9:00am. Occupying one of the most comfortable spots in the bus, I look through the window. Watching familiar places passing by and being left behind, my mind switches to a different channel. Even with my eyes still widely open, I do not see the world outside the window anymore. Instead, I see images stored in my mind, images from the last couple of days, mixed with imaginary pictures of what am I going to see in Africa. I lose touch with reality. The reflection of someone's suitcase on the window becomes the only stable and unquestionable point around me: an escape from an accelerating life that still has a lot to disclose for me. At some point, I dive deep into the philosophy of existence that I fall asleep.

A couple of bumps; bus slowing down; I must be arriving at the Chicago airport.

I wake up. Now it's time to unload the bags, find the checkpoint, and get food. Those are the main tasks for the next hour. I do all of it like a programmed computer, and even though there are still over three hours until boarding, I feel like there is not much time left. But if I think more... it is three hours... just three hours of being on the ground in the United States before leaving for three weeks of unknown Kenya.

Three hours seem to be only a split second then.

I like airports. I always did. Maybe I like them because my dad used to take me there when I was little. Maybe it is because his job of a pilot always evoked a sense of inspiration and excitement among others, or maybe because it is just a unique place. A place where people rush, travel for long distances in just a couple of hours, a place full of lost, anonymous tourists whose millions of faces pass by me, faces that I will not even remember. These are faces that seem to be sketched by an artist in a hurry. Faces are just a hologram, an unclear image hanging in the air.

I expect longer controls due to the orange level of security that was just announced. Finally, my luggage is checked-in and my carry-on controlled. Nothing made the gate beep.

Now the only thing left is to wait for boarding. However, in this particular context, waiting seems to be as difficult and tiring as all the other stages on the way to the Kenyan airport. I sit on the chair, next to other travelers who make themselves comfortable, resting in what appears on the outside to be a lazy pose.

6:05pm adding twenty-five minutes of delay.

The doors finally open. I enter the plane and find my spot where I am about to spend the next six hours. The flight is quite comfortable, with the smiling faces of the plane crew that either really cares, or makes the effort to look like it does. Good food and snacks, personal TV, radio and game site. Good seat. First impression: not bad. It should go by fast. I catch some sleep. Compared to all the other times when I crossed the ocean, this flight is quite good. I don't even feel tired. My neck hurts a little bit, but it starts to go away. In 1.5 hours, I will be in London. I try to catch some more sleep. There is no time for fatigue. Only half of the trip to Nairobi is over and half is left.

A couple more minutes pass. I look through the window again. A carpet of clouds below me looks like mountains hidden under the cover of snow. An artificial ground gives me the impression that I am not very high, but that is just an impression. 11000 meters is a lot, and it seems like those cozy formations are to help me feel safer. Finally, I see them begin to spread out, become diluted and disappear; a sea of milk is no longer there. Like an illusion, untouchable, and impossible to catch white formations revealed the water beneath. It was a flat, blue surface, looking quiet and peaceful, reflecting the sun, but twice as deep as the altitude I am at right now.

May 9, 2007

Europe. Here I am again. Not for long though. Arriving at 7:00 in the morning, I spend over 30 minutes more in the plane like travelling together for six hours with over 200 passengers was not long enough.

London. Great Britain from the air looks like any other European country. From the ground, I could tell exactly where I am. Leaving the plane, getting to the right terminal, going through check-in again, looking for information, all had to be done in relatively short time. But among it all, somewhere deeper, a shy little feeling of excitement, of being so close to my home country, starts to emerge but slowly and gently like it is afraid that if it revealed itself in full, all that has happened so far would disappear.

After several hours of waiting, I enter the plane to Nairobi. After I get comfortable and go through the list of movies that are offered, I decide that the view outside my window would be better than the efforts of directors. So I look: below me there are mountains. Amazing mountains with tops still covered with snow and sharp ridges emerging from the ground.

Dangerous, hostile…

…but mysterious and pretty.

I close my eyes...

...and open them. Next thing I see is a desert.

The African desert! Sahara!

I must have slept for quite some time since the European mountains and African desert do not lie next to each other. When I look down at the reddish sand, I still can't believe it. It feels like my window is just a TV screen, showing a geographical documentary. But no, the jet engine and right wing of the plane is also in the picture, persistently reminding me that I am on my way to Nairobi. I can see a beautiful sunset, and finally, it gets dark. As I fly over the continent, I could not see anything. No lights.

Nothing.

The black land seems to open its mouth, and I can only imagine what is down there. About fifteen minutes before landing, I see the city and little lanes made of street lamps, here and there are some lights in the buildings.

The plane lands!

I go through customs and baggage claim.

All done!

I am here! I am in Nairobi!

The baggage claim area is quite empty. I guess our plane is the only one that arrives at this time.

The peacefulness changes as soon as I enter the area where people are allowed. A lot of Kenyans come to greet and welcome the group I came with. A lot of emotions fill the air. In between of introductions, I find my way outside the building. The noise is still loud, but I realize that it is the excitement that makes an impression that all of Kenya came to welcome us.

After everyone's luggage is packed into the van, I take a spot in one of the cars and I am taken to the hotel where the rest of the team was staying for the next couple of days. As soon as they unloaded their baggage, I move again. This time the stop is in the house of a Kenyan family. It's late at night. Not the best road I have ever seen, leads me through the forest and empty suburbs to an amazing house, hidden behind a big fence, like a pearl in the shell of an ordinary mussel, amazes me with its beauty.

Welcomed with open hands and lots of warmth in the heart of the hosts, I smiled. It is a friendly surrounding, and makes me feel accepted and cared for. After dinner, I find rest in a bed, the first time since I left Anderson.

May 10, 2007

Someone is calling my name.

Once,

twice ...

five times.

Finally, a towel lands on me. I can hear a laugh. I open my eyes, just wide enough that I can see the outside world. I am woken up by my friend two hours before I actually need to get up.

Is this a Kenyan tradition? No, it's Emily. I try to get back to sleep but I can't. The birds singing outside and people moving around in the house help me wake my mind and get up.

I go to the kitchen, and seeing how the breakfast is being made I want to help.

I cook food.

Real Kenyan food!

Well, maybe "cooking" is too much, but I definitely help to prepare it.

In between making chapatis, I go outside. The weather and the surroundings are great. I try to catch every minute of this world that seems to be so elusive. With closed eyes and the wind gently touching my skin I listen to the noise the birds make. Exotic trees, exotic birds, exotic noises, all of them are now so close, so touchable. Sitting in front of the house, I know I am the only one from the whole group that is awake.

Occasionally going back to the kitchen to help cook, my mind is crossed by the thought that maybe I should go back to sleep. After all, I am tired from travelling. However, my friend told me: "let them sleep. Everyone works on their own on the way they want to be remembered here". How true is that! I don't want to sleep in anymore and I go back to help prepare breakfast. The pile of chapatis is growing bigger and bigger every second, even though I manage to add more to the pile only every few minutes. That's how long it takes me to make it as perfect as the ones that are already there.

It begins to warm up. At this time of year, it's winter here, or the rainy season, however the temperature still oscillates between 20-30 Celsius. The morning was chilly, but now I can feel the sun's rays on my back, telling me to take off my jacket.

I sit in front of the house again, looking at the blue sky and the moving clouds. It is so peaceful and quiet. For a moment, I feel like I am sitting on the porch of my grandparents' house during summer. The same feeling, the same weather, the same looking sky, and that's all that is the same. I am in Nairobi, Kenya... in a different part of the world.

It is around noon and time to visit the other part of the group in Grace - the hotel they stayed in. I have to bring them back to the house for lunch. I walk over there and, it is the first time I see the hotel and the garden in daylight. The tall palm trees and hanging garlands of flowers look amazing. The little artificial waterfall on the side of the building fills the landscape but on the other hand, looks very out of proportion. A few impressive predator birds circle above my head, looking for small rodents. This, combined with the unique scent of water from the pool and flowers, gives me an impression of some imaginary land, something on the border of dream and reality.

I find everyone outside gathered close to the pool, taking pictures, or talking in small groups. After many greetings and listening to the stories from last night, I invite them for lunch.

As we begin to walk back to the house, we pass a variety of hotels that seem to be springing from the ground on every corner of the street, growing bigger and taller, and showing off their distinctive architecture.

But as impressive as the buildings are, the fences also show the creativity of their owners. Most of them have an electric wire on top, some with broken glass stacked at the edge of high cement walls that don't appear very protective but much more interesting. However, one of the fences in particular captures my attention, being made entirely of plants, becoming a security guard and an art form at the same time: Cyprus trees and palms with sharp trunks are the majority of plants, making the fence impossible to cross. It is thick and green, looking nice, but thousands of thorns scream: "don't touch".

And as if all that is not enough, every two meters, a less careful walker could stab himself with lots of needles sticking out of the big cacti.

Time is going by really slowly. After dinner and several group pictures, I "broaden my horizons" in the YaYa Shopping Center where I spend most of the time writing a long email to my parents.

Leaving the brightness of the mall at about 7:30pm, I enter darkness. Night in Kenya comes quickly and is very dark. Not able to see anything, but with all my other senses strengthened, I am not sleepy anymore. The gentle noise of insects, buzz in my head. I am heading home where I find rest after a long day.

May 11, 2007

Here it comes. The big day!

Not the only one during this trip. I wake up, grab breakfast and wait to leave for Kibera – one of the world's biggest slums. To get there, the taxi drives through downtown. I see numerous modern buildings: hotels, banks, corporations. Palm trees separate glass and steel in a humble combination.

Kenya is full of that.

There is traffic on the streets. Strings of cars wait in a row to move toward their destination. Old Peugeots, new Mercedes and all ages of Land Rovers flood the street with virtually no noise, or honking in the city centre. In the chaos of driving and street blockades, nobody gets annoyed, nobody hates anyone for not leaving a space to pass through, or maybe they just hide it, hiding it well enough that I cannot see it.

Finally, I reach Kibera. Walking down the narrow path between the streets and crowds of people, my heart gets heavy. Inhabitants live here in extreme, unspeakable poverty. I see mud shacks that house more than seven people, no electricity, unhygienic living conditions due to lack of running water and trash collecting on the sides. No words can describe it. No one can imagine this poverty until they step down here and walk the path these people walk every day. Among the dirt and the sad shelters, I find thousands of smiling and friendly faces that look back at me. These are faces full of hope for a better future.

As I keep on walking I see kids running around, saying "how are you" to everyone who is new to them.

The children of Kibera are the most moving picture.

Too innocent to be here, too young to experience poverty,

Already too mature to be mother and father for each other.

The elders are nodding their heads, and the youth are playing around. It is like a bee hive, an overcrowded place where time runs at its own speed and where people enjoy life like they are unaware of how they could live if they were more fortunate.

Astonishing, amazing, touching, memorable, intense, transforming, moving: this is how one could describe what I see.

With thoughts still buzzing in my head, already having too much knowledge to absorb, I reach the Clinic - Frepals Nursing Home: an old, two-story building among dirty shacks.

The "welcome room" is a small cell with a couple of chairs and a desk. The paint is peeling off the wall. I feel some chocking sadness in the air. At the door, Freda Anani, a wonderful person who founded and maintains the clinic, a lady with a friendly smile and lively shining eyes. She seems to be an odd figure that does not fit the picture I have in front of me. Freda spent her pension to establish the clinic that would provide medical help to people from the Kibera community. She and her husband Paul gave up their private life to do good for others. No government or organization is sponsoring them, all medicines and equipment are bought with their own money. They do not get anything in return,

other than love from people. Medicines and costs of service are very cheap, only about $7, yet people often don't pay since they are not able to. Surprisingly, but fortunately, the Clinic is still working.

The conditions are terrible: no sheets on the beds, a lack of medical equipment, old, broken closets, and stains on the wall. Freda struggles to make ends meet and still provides help to those who need it. There are no words that can describe it. All what I see before my vision, when it is not blurred by tears that are passing down on my face like raindrops on the window, fills me with astonishing knowledge about this place, great sadness and a desire to help.

The needs of this place are bottomless; A heart may break when one sees how loving these two people are among the hardship but with no lack of hope.

At the end of the tour around the clinic, Freda and Paul have a surprise. A meal that they prepared is waiting. I am moved. Sitting in an empty room with only one table and a few chairs, I watch the pots and plates being brought in. The ugali, chicken, and two side dishes are great, but taste even more remarkably because of being prepared with so much heart. As we eat, we also talk about the university I go to, about my plans for the future, and about their

hopes and dreams. It is a memorable moment.

The time to walk back comes too quickly. It is raining. The sky is also crying over the fate of Kibera, and even though it stops right before I begin to head back, the path is difficult to bear. While on the way to the Clinic the paths were usable but have now become a challenge. Like with an invisible hand, the land keeps my feet, not letting me escape from that place. I try to walk slowly so as not to slip, but at the same time, fast to get to better paths.

This balance is hard to manage.

Passing faces again, elders, adults and kids. Crowds of very young children surround me again trying to grab my hand. They look at me, full of hope and joy, with their big, dark, onyx-like eyes. Four-year-olds are carrying one-year-olds on their backs.

Too innocent to be here…

…yet they are here, probably without any prospects for a better future.

Slipping and sliding, getting dirty all over, I struggle to walk. Someone behind me says, "white people do not understand mud." I think it is true. I am not ready for Kibera. No pictures or stories could have made me ready. Having lived all my life in comfortable conditions, I won't ever be able to understand people from Kibera until I live with them.

I am changed, I want to do as much as I can to know these people and help them. If I cannot make everyone happy, I can try, or at least make one person's life better.

I am determined.

Trying never hurts, they say.

I feel like I am equipped well enough now not to give up. Everyone can do big things. Sometimes, the quietest person can make the biggest change. A small rock thrown into the water leaves longer lasting circles on the surface than a big rock.

Let's do small things that will build up on each other and make a better future for everyone. What I have seen and what I have heard has changed me.

May 12, 2007

A familiar smell of food is reaching me: mandazis. I have to wake up. In two hours I am supposed to be on my way to Kericho. I eat breakfast, shower, and pack. I soon discover that my trousers and shoes have been cleaned from mud and clay from Kibera. The household I am staying in is a good experience. I have to leave for a week, but I will be back here. As the small buses – called matatu - start their engines, I become glued to the window, pulling my camera out in case I want to take a picture of what I see outside.

The drivers must have amazing skills from what I could see during frequent brave but risky maneuvers of turning into the proper lane right in front of an approaching car. The first couple of times, my eyes enlarge in fear. The speed is worthy

of attention too. It feels like a race but a different type. Being in a closed box, full of people squishing each other and running over holes and bumps in the street is quite a strenuous experience. With my head hitting the roof, I wonder how many bruises I am going to have after this ride.

Amazing views pass by my window, stunning me.

I do not want to blink, afraid that I may miss some outstanding landscape or event. Wonderful forests, canyons, cliffs, lakes, hills - so diverse, so awe-inspiring. Some abandoned houses are scattered in random places, being a persistent reminder that man's presence has marked this area.

As I am fed with the pictures coming up in front of my eyes, I am anxiously waiting to see animals. I do not need to wait long. A zebra, standing at a close distance from the road, does not seem bothered by cars passing by. Not even bothered by the scream I make spotting the animal. So much excitement over seeing an animal that, for locals, is not unique in any way. Gazelles, antelopes, warthogs are here too, so far available only in zoos, now become more realistic in the wild.

A few hours of driving have passed. Finally, I spot something odd on the right side of the road far in front of me: a thin silver string that seems to grow

Daria Barwinska

thicker in width as I approach. It is Lake Naivasha glittering in the sun. It looks almost surreal but beautiful.

The trip from Nairobi to Kericho takes about eight hours instead of the predicted four. The condition of the roads is more than bad. The bumps and holes not only delay the arrival at Kericho but also result in a couple of big bruises on my legs.

Night comes fast. Being still on the road becomes tiring and brings a kind of nervousness and concern, as with the outside getting darker, safety is decreasing. I finally arrive in the city, heading straight to the Kenya Highlands Bible College (KHBC). I am tired, but at the same time, I do not really mind driving more. After spending more hours in the matatu than on the trans-Atlantic flight, I begin to get used to it, as well as the bumps. However, laying my body on the bed under the mosquito net in one of the KHBC dorms feels like a blessing. It does not take me long to fall asleep.

May 13, 2007

Still tired, I wake up. Laughs and loud talking girls from the dorm reach my ears. It is 7:00 am. I know breakfast is supposed to start three hours later. I choose to lie on my bed, listening to the flow of words in the language I could not understand, Kiswahili. About 30 minutes pass and I decide to get ready for the day. I have breakfast in one of the dining courts, and then a small tour around campus.

The day seems to go by slowly, and I spend most of it resting after the bumpy trip here. I walk around the area and realize I am in a country where I can have natural juices from the most tropical and exotic fruits I can only imagine. Mango, pineapple,

and passion fruit are just a few of the many options. I look at the watch. It is 10:00 am.

Sunday morning, to about one third of the world's population, means church service. Starting at 11:00 am, it lasts a little bit less than two hours. Full of glory and genuine faith, the people who gather here with open hearts, impress me.

The church resembles a barn back home in Poland that someone transformed into the house of God. Even though it is poor, the spirit of this community lifts it high above many churches I have experienced so far.

It is easy to dive into this community of hospitable people and never want to come back. Is it even possible to live alongside these fully tolerant people and not give in to the allure of Kenya?

After lunch, in the home of another Kenyan family, I return to KHBC and having some free time, I decide to take a walk, this time outside the campus.

Time passes by, especially during the far walk toward the city centre. Not even half way there, I see an Islamic mosque and decide to stop. Not allowed to enter, I wander around, getting my white trousers dirty with red clay. I decide to return to campus for dinner.

I spot, what looks like abandoned houses. Little children are running around to hide themselves in some shelter where they can see me without being seen. The air is filled with the scent of ginger and wet grass. I see a forest in the horizon, millions of trees of different sizes and shapes. All this combine to make a landscape full of peaceful harmony.

I have to go to chapel, and then I have dinner. It is a good time. Having my fifth cup of chai* today, I decide to stay up playing a card game called Uno. What a different end to the day.

*Chai is the local tea, tea leaves, milk and water are boiled together and served very hot sometimes pre-sweetened with plenty of cane sugar. If there is a national drink for Kenya it is chai. Served most any time of day, and for any occasion, it became a game to count the daily cups.

May 14, 2007

I wake up right on time to get ready and not be late for breakfast. As I run down the stairs, I feel sunrays on my shoulder. It's going to be a nice day. Breakfast: bread and chai, as usual.

Full of desire to see the surroundings of the campus, I go on another small field trip. Walking the thin path hidden among tall grass, I reach the little gate at the back of campus. I pass through it, at the same time entering a much wider path leading down the hill. As I walk there, I pass the banana plantation. Very short plants, with disproportionally big leaves, cover the area on the right. I stop and look through the fence. Heavy bunches of bananas are hanging from every single plant, bringing it down to the soil.

To Be... in Africa

From those bunches there are hanging reddish/violet formations, which turn into bananas later, but are now only pulling the already existing ones down.

I keep walking, passing a little elementary school and reaching a cliff with a little lake below. Struggling to get as close as I can, I get dirty again, but it is worth the view. In front of me I have a picturesque view of mango trees and tall grass. I climb back up the cliff and, feeling like I need to change my clothes, decide to head back to campus. I do not quite make it there before it rains. Initially, it is drizzling a little bit, but as soon as I enter the gate, it starts to pour down like from a bucket.

I am soaked.

I really need to shower.

2:00 pm. After a lunch composed of the usual rice and beans, I visit one of the classes. It turns out to be a Public Relations Lecture. Eleven Kenyan students are diligently taking notes, listening to the professor. At the end a few of them ask questions or share views. However, there is a kind of quietness among the people gathered.

It seems odd, different from what I am used to.

It looks like it is all staged. It is all good, but tense in a way. It is like a mutual respect that is transforming into some kind of barrier that neither side wants to cross. I leave the classroom still thinking about the lecture and the way it was carried out. In about 5 minutes later I find myself back in my room. I feel my head getting heavy so I decide to take a nap. Later in the afternoon it is still raining. The walking paths around become difficult to use. The slowness of the day and the rain make me want to stay in bed, but I have to get up. It is time for dinner.

As I get to the cafeteria, everyone else is already there. I go to get my portion of food and take a place opposite a young Kenyan student that I met the day before. We talk for a moment, being interrupted by big flying ants that are attracted to the light and entered the room through semi-open doors. Time goes by fast. I head back to the dorm, taking small steps and enjoying the fresh air of the night.

May 15, 2007

I hear a noise…

…louder and louder.

Still dreaming, I begin to realize it is real. Finally, I am awake and back to reality. The girls living in the dorm talk in Kiswahili and get ready for class. It is 7:40 in the morning. Breakfast starts at 10:00 am. I have over two hours to get ready and figure out how to spend the rest of the day productively.

I decide that doing laundry would be a good idea, considering I started to run out of shirts.

I have a cup of hot chai, and then another. I feel a little congested, and my throat is sore. This is not how I want it to be. Thankfully, my mom, who is a nurse, taught me how to get better. Remembering the familiar smell of the hospital that she always brought home after work, I was getting inspired by the medical wisdom. Now, being always prepared for almost every situation, I take some medicine and hurry to chapel to practice the ministry show that I am a part of.

The chapel goes well. I now have lunch and the long awaited trip to the tea factory in Kenya Highlands. I enter the bus that arrived few minutes late, and I am on my way there. Finally, I arrive. As I pass through the gate, I begin moving across the tea plantation. The amount of land covered with little tea bushes is breathtaking. Endless carpets of tea cover every hill and every possible strip of land that is not used for any other purpose. There are oceans of little plants. Wherever the eyes can reach - everywhere is tea. The green blanket is cut by little dark passages where one can spot Kenyan workers in bended poses and big baskets on the back. It looks like a maze you can get lost in. How interesting it would be to get lost among the greenness of the best drink in the world.

After about 40 minutes of driving, I reach another gate. This time it is the factory complex. Greeted by the major in-charge, I begin my tour inside. After

Daria Barwinska

washing my hands and disinfecting my shoes, I can enter the building. Several workers are putting bags full of tea on the lift that carries them to the cutting place. But before that, the leaves are dried by big fans spinning clockwise or anti-clockwise, depending on the conditions outside, sucking in or out the moist air. If the humidity is higher outside than inside, the air is being sucked out of the leaves, but if it is not as humid but hotter outside, then the air is pumped in. All this is done to dry the leaves faster.

Like big meat minces, machines cut the leaves that are thrown inside it like a food to the throat of a big creature. There are several cutting stages, each yielding more of the mushy green substance. Now, this not so very moist mass enters another phase. This time, passing through magnets and fans, making sure metal, glass and other unnecessary dust is removed; it reaches the drying phase called oxidation or fermentation.

Slowly the green mass starts to turn brown, heated from below. The air is now saturated with the smell of tea, not leaves any more, but black tea, the one you buy from the store. But that is not the end of processing. They still need to pull out fibers, sort tea according to the size of the particles, and pack the bags ready for export. The factory employs over

18,000 workers, is self-sustainable, and provides over 75% of the energy needed. It has its own woods, houses for employees and schools for their children. Medical aid for families is also available.

The tea plantation is amazing, like a city within a city. On the way back, I try to grasp the last moments of this place in Kericho. Later that evening, I have a dinner at the house of one of the professors at KHBC, games, and obligatory chai.

An evening filled with cascades of rain.

May 16, 2007

Squeaks, loud noises like from a workplace. What is happening? I wake up suddenly not knowing how I should interpret the sound and what I should do? Lying in my bed trapped under the mosquito net, I listen more carefully. Finally, I come up with an interpretation, which I will never know if it is correct because I never check. However, I choose to think that a girl in the next cell is moving her big, heavy, metal bed around scratching the floor. A little bit calmed down now, I get up.

I have breakfast. Soon after that, in a hurry I pack clothes and necessities I need to take to Kisumu.

I have 1.5 hours to pack. 11:30 a.m. – the group to Uganda has just left with a delay, I begin heading to Kisumu. Again images start to cross my mind like a documentary. I think how many plants grow here in the wild that I have in pots at home. I see a beautiful lily pollinated by hummingbirds, happening so fast that it is difficult to spot. I see a variety of birds and a variety of plants. The travel takes a few hours. As I arrive at Kisumu, I crave for food. The options are either the restaurant at the hotel, or a local shack at the lake where they serve fried fish, tilapia and Nile perch, straight from the water.

Full of desire to experience Kenyan culture in total, I choose the shack. Getting from the city downtown to the fish market takes about 5 minutes. The arriving bus attracts the owners of the food places to gather around. Before I even leave the vehicle, they try to convince me to pick the particular spot to eat.

Lots of people…

Lots of voices - almost ordering me where to eat…

Lots of hands pushing me in different directions…

It could be quite overwhelming for some.

Finally, I sit down in one of the restaurants with a view of Lake Victoria and bushes in the

background. I see people playing in the water and some inhabitants that seem to spend all their lives observing tourists, or maybe tourists just do not show up here often enough and those who do are sort of a local attraction.

The place itself is just a roof on a sandy, stony floor covered with clay and pieces of food. Old, cheap tables and chairs indicate that a lot of people have been dining here. The air is soaked with the smell of fried fish, making me even hungrier. A little concerned about the sanitary conditions, I decide to go with the flow. I am hungry, and after all, I had decided to come here to experience the culture.

Soon, a lady with long red nails pulls me over to the fish stand so I can choose the fish that will be prepared for me. On the big display board are fresh tilapia and Nile perch caught a moment ago. With their eyes gazing at me, I feel like a barbaric carnivore. I do not see a difference in any of the fish shown; they all have the same size, color and sad eyes. I need to overcome the feeling of moral doubts and sympathy. Balancing the nearly wild instinct of a meat eater with simple hunger and curiosity, I am ready for lunch to come. I do not wait long. The fish, as well as chapati are ready in less than 15 minutes.

Served on a big plate with no cutlery, I use my hands.

The fish is great.

Even though my tongue is burned I keep putting little hot white pieces of meat into my mouth. Occasionally interrupted by random sellers trying to convince me that I need another safari hat, I finish eating. I am glad I came here!

On the way back, I look again at the lake. I spot a kingfisher waiting patiently in the air for a fish that would come close to the surface. A couple of bigger birds – some predators – are also circulating around looking for small mammals.

I get back to the city centre. Walking down the crowded street, encouraged by street sellers to buy their products, I spot an internet café - time to send a note home.

I am back in the matatu and back on the bumpy road. I finally arrive in KIST (Kenya International School of Theology), welcomed by the missionaries who live and work here. Originally from the United States, they have spent already five years in Kenya. Having dinner, unexpectedly American…

…I crave for chapattis and chai.

I feel tired after the whole day of traveling and excitements. Finding peace and refuge in an empty house that belongs to other missionaries, I take a warm shower. How relaxing. It is surprising how small things can make someone happy.

Later that night, my itinerary is changed again (I have already begun to get used to the unplanned events) by delaying the bed time and engaging into a half-fun, half-serious discussion with the school nurse. Beginning it with talking about diarrhea, we finish it discussing the purpose of life. I start yawning. It is time to sleep. I say goodnight and go to bed. It was a good talk. I enjoyed it, and I think that everyone else who was there did too.

May 17, 2007

I couldn't sleep last night. When I feel like I finally caught some sleep, I have to wake up. 7:30 am. Too early for breakfast and it's raining outside, additional motivation to stay in bed.

After a few minutes I choose to lift myself up.

Again, a non-Kenyan meal was prepared by the hosts, which is a little disappointing, since I had been expecting some African cuisine. Then I have a little tour on campus at KIST and visit of one of the classes.

The lecture I go to is more of a debate. A very intense debate ensued. Full of enthusiasm, students argue about the righteousness of donations for the

African Church. The air is soaked with real tension even though it is only a class assignment. Cooling down at the missionaries' house after the vivid discussion, I wait endlessly for chapel to begin.

As I sit on the couch, engaging myself in the conversation with the hosts, I find out things that surprise me and that I would not expect to hear from people who are expected to be supportive of the culture and also care for the students that they are supervising. My image of missionaries changes drastically, as I have in front of my eyes an example how far from the ideal things can be. Time is passing by, even faster as my heart starts racing due to the new findings and revelations. Another chapel is approaching fast, as well as another brainstorming on what to present.

Introductions, a song, it is looking to be an ordinary event. However, soon it is transformed into a deep and meaningful experience for the KIST students but also for me.

The opening by Ray Martin, Scott's father, who already has a rich past in Kenya, touches me a lot. His speech is uplifting and refers to truths that I have realized myself and that I also carry in my heart. Listening to him made me stronger, and solidified my passions and determination to fight for what I stand for and to help those who need it; to never give up, even if life puts a lot of obstacles.

There is always hope, and with enough strength everything can be overcome. I believe I have enough strength in me. My passions are strong, like a fire that burns but brings a renewing of the earth.

Feeling very uplifted and empowered; I begin to settle my dreams and motivate myself to listen to the speech carried out by Scott. His words made my eyes water, not only because his words themselves were moving, but because I could personally relate to what he was saying.

Unlimited empathy.

"When the smells, tastes, sights, and sounds remind me of myself, I know I am home." I think about my home in Poland, and how I felt when I arrived there 1.5 years after being away. But I also think about Kenya. Even though the smells, sights, sounds and tastes are new, they have become a part of me now.

Kenya is my home too

...another one, because, to me, home is a place where you find those that you care for.

I leave the building. Thoughts are spinning in my mind. Walking back, I meet somebody, a short man with a little afro on his head, about 40 years old, wearing a red shirt and jeans, and carrying a file folder of an enormous size. His face is shining with friendliness. Smart and big eyes widely open attract and evoke my curiosity. He shakes my hand and smiles. His smile is warm, full of peace and quietness. He is the great-grandson of Haile Selassie, a great emperor of Ethiopia. A wonderful little man, small in stature but big in heart and history.

In the afternoon, I head back to KHBC, stopping on the way by a small village where I get some souvenirs.

May 18, 2007

It has rained for days, cascades of water.

Sitting in the room, I look through the window. It is wet all over, and does not look like it was going to stop anytime soon. The sun is hidden behind big clouds. I look closer. Drops of water are dripping from a big leaf next to the window. No one is outside. Campus looks deserted. Roads are unusable. Several cars stuck in the mud were abandoned by their owners who hurried to their homes to wait for the rain to stop.

When it rains, it seems like life stops, nothing that lives and can move is outside. The world is still,

only the rain drops play a symphony of sounds on the roofs and puddles.

Rain looks like tears, but it also washes out, cleans, redeems, maybe that's why it is believed in Kenya to bring good luck.

I do nothing the whole day.

Spending hours in front of the window, I become hungry. Since the planning this day had not been great, the scheduled lunch never happens. I have to take care of it by myself, going to the city downtown, risking getting stuck in the mud. I am with three more people in the car. As we drive down, I see other drivers struggling to keep the car going. Fortunately, I manage to get there and get back on campus without any major problems, carrying a bag full of food.

I eat fast.

I decide to spend the rest of my day in the same spot in front of the window. A few hours later at around 4:00pm, it stops raining for a while. Students and faculty emerge from their shelters for the ceremony of tree planting. A tree in honor of the relationship with Anderson University is planted on the KHBC campus. I also go down there. The grass is wet, the path is muddy, and I am cold. Shaking, I stand there for a couple of minutes until I notice a little chameleon crawling on the hand of one of my friends. It is tiny and green, even though it looks shy at first; it walks confidently ahead until it reaches the finger tip. I take it into my hand.

Interesting creature.

The tree is planted and the ceremony ends. It is still light outside, but looks like it wants to rain again. I head back for an early chai. One of seven I have today! This time I sit at the fireplace, beginning to get tired of constantly looking into the window, where the view has not changed since this morning.

I play with the orange furred cat that comes to me to lie on my lap. Making noises that mean satisfaction in its life, it falls asleep.

How can I move?

I don't.

I stay there for an hour, flying away with my thoughts and getting sleepy too.

May 19, 2007

8:00 am. Breakfast. I have been ready since 7:00 in the morning. Ready and very awake. The day appears to be sunny, even though it is still early morning, I can feel sunrays on my skin, getting stronger, and almost burning.

Having two options for today, I decide to go downtown, taking two of my friends. The other option is to wait for the rest of the group and then go downtown, a couple of hours later. I do not want to spend half of my day inside again. I expect the day to be really pretty, and I want to see the town. There are two ways that I can get to downtown: one is along the road, which goes around the campus, so it is the longer way, and the other - the "shortcut" is through the field and little village. I take the "shortcut" and begin penetrating through the tall grass, struggling to walk on a muddy path, almost falling and slipping all the time. I feel like the local people look at me as if I am some odd piece of a puzzle that does not really fit into the world they know. I also feel like that. I must look really helpless trying to walk confidently and like one of them, trying not to look like a tourist not used to these conditions. But I must not be very good at it. I am struggling.

Long grass, thick bushes, slick road. Not easy. This makes me to walk slower, therefore extending the time that I had hoped to spend on getting to the city centre. As if that is not hard enough, little baby goats playing around are catching my attention, making me stop from time to time to look at them.

Green and red.

Green grass and red clay are the dominant colors of this scene. Finally, I leave the village area, entering something that looks like a little jungle but with lower trees. Here, the journey becomes more difficult, as now I have to deal with mosquitoes, little plants with big needles and cliffs. It is easy to slip and fall, even get injured. I walk on the edges about a foot wide on the left side having a wall of soil and on the right hand having a steep slope down.

Exciting, thrilling, different from my usual life? Yes. Tiring? For sure!

Finally, I reach a fence that looks odd. This man-made wire creation in an area that looks like no man has ever been here just does not fit the picture. Soon, I discover what the fence is dividing me from: a dump. The only way to get out of this bushy and slick place is through a dump! Theoretically, I could also just go back to the campus, but tired after all that effort of getting here and still hoping to get to the city before noon; I do not want to give up. I decide to face it! At first, it is not that bad. I step on papers and foil bags all dry from the sun. If I do not look down, I would think I am stepping on solid ground, asphalt-like, but then the real extreme comes later.

I finally begin to smell the place. Maybe this is because it is not just paper and bags anymore. This is a real dump, with old shoes, food, and who knows what else. It is soaked. With great effort, I try to find a dry spot to step on. I am doing quite well until I miscalculate.

As I try to cross the little ditch filled with dirty water, I step on something that looks reliable enough to step on. It is just an illusion. As a result my leg ends up knee-high in the brown, wet dirt.

I think I will throw up.

I roll up my jeans, but it does not bring me much of a better feeling. I still feel that stuff in my shoes but have no chance to clean it.

The smell is unbearable.

I have to cover my nose.

I try a second time. I step into the stinking water again. I do not care anymore. I just want to get out of here. I start running faster, not paying attention to where I am stepping. Even if I get dirtier, well that would not be a whole lot worse than how I look and smell now.

Flies are everywhere. Like in a mad act of courage and strength, I climb the hills of trash to get out of this place. I finally do.

Exhausted, I find myself back on the road. I walk a couple more miles and decide to stop. I sit on a stone nearby catching my breath and thinking how to clean myself. Who would think I would end up in a car-wash – the only place close enough where I could ask for running water?

I can imagine it must be an unusual sight for the workers seeing me wash my legs under some little tap.

I feel better now but not good enough.

I hope to get new shoes in the city since mine are soaked and walking in them is quite funny. As I reach downtown I enter the first store that I see and get only new socks, but that is better than nothing. And anyway, after a while of walking I dry so I do not want to mess with my pants or shoes anymore. No need to add that the "shortcut" turned out to be a longer and more "extreme" way.

Walking the narrow streets of Kericho is a whole lot different from Nairobi. Not only in terms of the size of the city and the modernity, or maybe Western look of Nairobi, but also in terms of the attitude of the locals. Almost nobody pays attention to a white Western person wandering around in Nairobi. In Kericho, I feel I have become an attraction for those who live here. I realize there may not be very many tourists that arrive here. This is an odd collection of narrow streets, narrow pavements, small short buildings, mostly restaurants and bars, some stores selling accessories for cars, and some selling clothes. Crowds of people rest outside watching the pedestrians pass by; I imagine day by day with the same expression, like they have been sewn to the plastic chairs they sit on.

Little kids run around, trying to play hide and seek with me, but I am not hiding, so they play for themselves, hiding and watching me, trying to remain unnoticed.

It is hot; dusty roads and dry air make me thirsty. I stop by a store to get a soda. A few minutes later and less than a mile, I meet one of the ladies teaching in KHBC. We wander for a bit more, sit down and talk.

All this time, I am in full-sun so I look at my arms. They are red. I know I have a sun burn and the next day it is going to be painful. It is already too late. My sunscreen must not have been strong enough, or I must not have used it as diligently as I had thought.

A few minutes later, we resume our walk to the open-air market, something that is popular in Africa and some parts of Europe but almost never seen in the United States. Here in front of me is a big area of land covered by blankets or little primitive stands loaded with food. As soon as I cross the gate, I am hit by the intense smell of pineapples that is flowing in the air. Bananas, mangoes, pineapples, the most common fruit one could see here. Some vegetables, rice in big sisal bags sold per cup. Little dried fish piled in a mound that mixes the fruity smell in the air with its not very intense but surely different aroma.

Under a big aluminum roof that occupies the central part of the market, some people bring animals for sale: mostly chickens, but there are also some goats.

It is crazy. Pushed by people who want to get to the stands, I try to avoid falling and being run over by trucks which move at a high speed among the narrow paths between the stands, honking constantly to make people move to the side. It seems like a well coordinated, almost staged show, which requires great skill to carry it on since in this crowd nobody has gotten hurt.

I try to avoid ditches filled with rain water and food wastes, uneven paths leading from one sales stop to the other. The organized chaos is filled with multiple Kenyans shouting in Kiswahili into their cell phones. What a contrast. What a unique and thought-provoking picture.

I begin to walk back. This time, due to past experience, I take the longer, but in fact much more pleasant way along the road. Extremely exhausted, I get back on campus. I take shower. How relaxing, and above all, how refreshing.

I just have to do laundry now. One reason is that I have begun to run out of clean shirts, second reason is that the smell of my clothes after the journey downtown is unbearable and detectable from very far. I bought a bar of laundry soap for 10 Kenyan Shillings.

I filled two buckets with water. One, I use for wetting my clothes and cleaning the dirt, that's why the water turns dark quickly, and the foam almost comes out of it. The other, I use to rinse the clothes off right before hanging them on the ropes in the small yard, or rather laundry space in the dorm. I am exhausted after the trip downtown, and can barely squeeze any additional strength out of me to do the laundry. It is more physical work for today. With all the technology that I have at home, I must say that I realize how I am not used to the simple life. But at the same time, glad I have a chance to experience it. I have done hand-washing before, but it was never a routine activity.

To Be... in Africa

Later that day, I try to slow down, catch some rest. And I do a little bit. I still have to be a part of the Chapel at the KHBC, which actually turns out well, considering the fact that it is prepared almost a few hours before.

Sigh…another chai before I go to sleep.

I walk to my dorm. I look up at the sky. Beautiful stars. They seem so close. There are so many.

It's an amazing universe! I count myself lucky to be in it.

May 20, 2007

Sunday morning. It's really nice outside, and I feel rested, but my arms hurt. I can see how sun burnt I am. With my arms as pink as the tiles on the wall in my dorm room, I manage to get up and get dressed. The shirt I put on irritates my skin. Anything I put on would irritate my skin. Any touch, even the gentlest gives me a burning pain. At 10:00 am I go to the church, being led by a curiosity of how people worship in Kenya.

I am almost late to church. But I am not the only one. Apparently, Kenyan acceptance of being late extends even to the church, as I see many other locals entering the building much later than I did.

After the service, I decide to stick around and talk to some people, while exchanging a few words with the church members, my attention is drawn to a little group of about ten monkeys. They enter through the main gate and immediately spread into groups of two or three. Confidently walking around and figuring out the surroundings, gaining even more self-confidence, they begin to climb the cars that are parked by the fence. Jumping on the trunk and roof, to me they look joyful; however, it seems the locals perceive them as something little more than pests. A few of the monkeys remain at the gate, carefully observing the situation. I come closer, noticing that these two larger monkeys are not alone. I see their little ones hanging on to their fury chests and arms. Looking with curiosity and awe in their big black eyes; they are just amazing. So helpless, and shy, hiding among their mothers' arms, still pulling their heads up, trying to see the outside world, finding comfort in this warm cradle not ready to start independent life yet.

At around 1:00 pm I get back on campus for lunch. I do not pre-plan the rest of my day. That turns out to be quite a good idea for this lazy Sunday afternoon. The weather is great. Sunny but dry. Not many people around. It seems like everyone scheduled their naps for the same time of the day. I change my clothes, take a book with me and look

for a perfect spot to read, relax and enjoy the sun. I do not go far, ending up at the same place where I used to rest throughout my entire stay at KHBC: outside of the Administration building on one of the steps, right next to my dorm, in the center of campus.

I make myself comfortable, already enjoying the touch of the sun rays on my skin. I read about thirty pages from time to time, letting myself close my eyes and just listen to the sounds around me, or look around me, to see ibises walking on the lawn in front of me, or hummingbirds flying around little lilies on the right.

Sitting in the sun is great. I am warm and feel rested. However, soon this idyll becomes too idyllic, and my eyelids become too heavy. Slowly getting more and more sleepy, with my eyes irritated from the sunlight reflected from the white pages of my book, I begin to think about a nap. The warmth of the sun, the quietness around, and the general feeling of relaxation put me asleep. I walk back to my room, and give in to the blessed 2-hour nap under my mosquito net.

When I wake up, it is almost time to go to chapel and practice, with the Kenyan students, our final presentation.

The chapel turns out to be a success. Everyone enjoys it. I also think it went well.

Right after that, I crave for chai. Last one in KHBC. I drink only one cup, but slowly, enjoying every sip of this national drink, and thinking about the past week and the people that I met. Finally, at about 10:00 pm I go back to my dorm, thinking I will spend an hour packing before the next day, and go to sleep to get rest and be ready to wake up early to leave.

However, my plans do not go according to what I expected. Instead I am surprised by the girls from my dorm named Kilimanjaro, who have prepared a "farewell get-together." They make chai (so the one before is not the last one on campus), have gifts and tons of words of how grateful they are that I stayed with them in the same dorm, interacted and was able to just "be" with them.

A lot of beautiful words...

A lot of emotions...

A great surprise...

A great memory...

That night I go to sleep, not yet ready to leave.

May 21, 2007

I am in a room full of people. Some of them I know, but some are strangers. We talk, but I cannot recognize the language and topic. In the background, I hear other voices, getting louder and louder, the faces in front of me fade away and begin to disappear.

I wake up a little apprehensive of what is going on. I lie down for a bit until I realize what day it is, what time it is and what I need to do. I am leaving KHBC today. Straight from here I will go to Maasai Mara Game Park. But before, I need to shower and pack.

Brrr... cold water in the shower. It is not very pleasant but at least I refresh myself and become more alert. I pack the items on my desk: soap, shampoo, a pair of jeans and t-shirt from the day before. My towel is still wet, but I have to pack it too.

I get dressed and begin to pull my heavy luggage behind me toward the center of the campus where the bus is parked. This time, I am supposed to ride a bus for at least half of the way to Maasai Mara.

When I got here, tired and sweating again from the physical exercise I have had with my suitcase, everyone else is already here. All the students from KHBC, who are staying on campus, have come to say goodbye. We take a group picture. I exchange some more words with a few of them who I want to say bye to in a more personal way.

I don't like farewells. Some are just too pathetic, some are not enough, and all are sad. This one is not enough. It has been only a week at KHBC, but I have already gotten used to the people I met here. I made friends, I learned a lot. The wisdom of locals can be inspiring...

But the bus is waiting. For the first time since I came to Kenya, my transportation is actually on

To Be... in Africa

time. I pack my luggage, making noises and removing drops of sweat from my forehead, even though it is a relatively cool morning. A few minutes later, I am on my way to Maasai Mara with stop at Narok for lunch. As soon as the bus pulls over, I notice a few matatus are already waiting to take me on the second half of my trip to the game park.

Lunch is good. And I was hungry. I leave my luggage at Narok, since it would be a hassle to take the heavy load on a safari. I pack a few necessary items that I would need for the next three days and sit in one of the matatus.

I am on my way to Maasai Mara. As soon as I leave Narok, I see fewer and fewer buildings, the cities transform into villages to become a Maasai land with Maasai huts scattered all around, and Maasai cows roaming on the vast area of land. I see less and less of the "civilized" world, and more and more of pure nature. Finally, I begin to see animals; we must be quite a good distance from the city then.

The travel is rough. It is even rougher than the journey on the way to Kericho. From Nairobi to Kericho there were at least some relatively good parts of the road, while here; there are no apparent roads at all. The driver takes a path between two villages that is supposed to lead to the camp. He is not worried that the way looks like a challenge like one of those in reality shows in the Western world where people volunteer themselves to get sent to some hostile part of the world where they have to survive and find their way out in order to win. This looks similar. I would take another way, but he looks comfortable and confident enough to pass through. In front of us there is a ditch. A very big ditch filled with rain water. The matatu slows down, almost stopping in front of it. Then it moves back, getting the necessary distance for acceleration.

We wait a few seconds.

Then go!

Fast.

Faster.

Like a mad act, the driver moves the vehicle forward. But the matatu does not manage to make it to the other side. It sticks in the ditch behind.

Instantly, as if materializing from the brush, a few young Maasai men from the nearby village appear to help. They are followed by their wives and mothers who spend their time making jewelry, and trying to use the opportunity to sell their art.

After a few minutes of struggling with the vehicle and the muscles tensing of the men who pushed the matatu, I can continue my way to the camp at Maasai Mara.

I am amused by the driver's skills in finding the right direction. There are no roads, no signs. Any markings left by a human hand would probably disappear within a day, erased by the wildness of this region.

Yet, he drives in a way that looks like he knows where he is going, turning at particular moments, before or after particular trees. For me, it looks like roaming in the forest, however after five hours, I finally make it to the camp named Acacia. It is already dark. The beautiful sunset with multiple colors over the hill begin to darken and disappear on the night sky.

The camp is nice. The big modern zipped tents look safe and comfortable to sleep in.

It is getting darker and cooler outside to the point that I almost cannot see my own feet. I am getting hungry too. Finally dinner is served. The crew of the camp has prepared dinner for tonight. I cannot wait to start eating. It looks good, and tastes good too!

Rice, vegetables, beef stew and chapati.

I eat it under a big wooden, round roof covered with straw. In the middle of the table is a little gas lamp giving just enough light that I can see my plate.

After dinner, full and tired, I spend about an hour next to the bonfire that a Maasai started a few minutes before, watching it, not letting it go off. I go back to my tent at 11:00pm. I have to get up early the next day. I am lying under a red Maasai blanket still shivering from cold. I get up and put on another layer of clothes. I feel better. I lie down again. It is dark in the tent. My opened eyes try to find something to look at, but the darkness that surrounds me is impossible to penetrate, impossible to explore.

I close my eyes and begin to listen to noises. At night, when the air is clearer, sounds travel much better.

Hisses, squeaks, etc.

I hear it all very well. Some reach me from very far, some must be very close. I am in the centre of a wild area; a place that does not sleep, even at night; a place where night life is even more exciting and dangerous than during the day.

So vivid during the day...

so mysterious and reverent at night.

But death on safari is the same at any time. Prey dies for the sake of their executioners.

But maybe night makes it less barbaric, less brutal. There are no pictures. Nobody can see anything. Only hear. And even though sounds can be more thrilling, than pictures, the overall atmosphere is more mystique, like an eternal ritual of survival and hunting.

I listen to these noises. Noises of crying, calling, navigation and warning, until exhausted from it all, I fall asleep.

May 22, 2007

It's very cold. I'm tired, and I want to sleep, but I can't. Covered in a Maasai blanket, I am shivering. The tent insolates well from the outside but not well enough. In accompany with the chill, animals roaming at night, make the full symphony of nature.

I hear birds.

More birds. Finally, I begin to recognize also human sounds. The staff of the camp Acacia is making breakfast. The safari begins early in the morning when the animals are moving around in search for food. It's 8:00 am. Suddenly, the

To Be... in Africa

temperature begins to rise. The sun is higher too. That makes perfect sense.

On safari, there are no paved roads. The matatu struggles through the grass, hills, holes, ditches, ponds, still trying to follow the routes created by animals. I know I will be exhausted by the end of the day, constantly holding tight to the roof or little handles in the vehicle, I try to avoid bruising as much as I can.

The first exotic animal (exotic for me) that I spot is a giraffe. Standing still behind the bush harmonizing with the surrounding acacia tree seems just an illusion. Here I am across from this big marvelous animal with a long neck. Soon I notice that it is not alone. Further ahead, a whole bunch of them are having their breakfast in the first sunrays of the savanna sky. Standing peacefully, not even moving a bit, just chewing some leaves and looking at me with an uncaring look like it does not mind me watching it, and at the same time, it does not really care that I am there. After a while of this gaze of unseeing eyes, it turns its head and continues chewing. It looks like turning its head is the only attraction that is scheduled for the coming hour.

Some of the younger ones, further from me, enjoy the life playing with each other and running around.

However, a giraffe's run is different from what people would normally expect. Due to its long neck, it runs slower with its head swinging in the air. It all looks like slow motion, like someone recorded it and replayed the tape slowing down the run to almost unnatural speed.

Watching these animals feeding and moving around for fifteen minutes is exciting, but I move on to another part of the Maasai Mara Game Park.

As the matatu is moving along the narrow path, I look around, trying to find another animal, maybe a zebra, maybe an elephant, or some cheetah resting on the tree. But what I see goes beyond my wildest imagination. Behind the tree there is a lioness. I cannot see the front part of her body, but based on the way she is moving it looks like she is forcing with something. The vehicle drives around the tree to reveal what it is. A lioness eating, or rather cleaning what is left of a buffalo.

A thrilling picture.

I have never seen a buffalo before, but now one is lying in front of me. Dead. Its head is untouched, but the guts are gone. Ribs shooting far in the air like white columns that used to support the rest of the body. Eyes look at me, but no longer seeing.

Not feeling. There is not even a lot of blood around. Nothing is wasted in nature. There is just a big liver thrown behind, like it as something uneatable. But even this will be well used. If not by lions, then the jackals, or vultures, already waiting at some distance for the leftovers of this breakfast. The movements of the lioness aligned with the buffalo, sounds of tearing meat, chewing, swallowing. This saturation of the senses is less than three meters from me. Thrilling, scary but also empowering in a sense. I see all of nature in its vivid colors. I see the struggle for survival, the hunter and the prey. This is real life on the savanna, repeated everyday like in a circle.

Driving away I am still thinking about it, and about the power of nature and the power of the image. I look around, endless land, scattered trees. Far in the distance a herd of gazelles is roaming. I close my eyes. I realize how small and helpless I am; just a little human being in the middle of the savanna among the animals, among the purest essence of nature and its rules. What a powerful force that we all give into, subordinate to. Here is a place that has been driven by the same forces for ages; a place where one life means nothing. This is a place in perfect harmony.

Understanding.

To Be... in Africa

Survival of the fittest.

Humility… and pride.

All these terms swirl in my mind. I want to sit down, but I am still standing, wanting to see even more, and think about it more. I want to fill my mind and soul with the richness of this moment.

I become so humble, so respectful for what surrounds me and drives me.

As to go along with the scenario and moment, I remember one of the songs by Elton John. As I keep looking around me, I silently sang it in my head.

> "There's far too much to take in here
> More to find than can ever be found
> But the sun rolling high through the sapphire sky
> Keeps great and small on the endless round
>
> In the circle of life
> It's the wheel of fortune
> It's the leap of faith
> It's the band of hope
> Till we find our place
> On the path unwinding
> In the circle, the circle of life"*

Music by Elton John, lyrics by Tim Rice, Available on the soundtrack the Lion King

Still wandering away with my thoughts, I realize that I have traveled through quite a bit of the Maasai Mara Game Park. I get back down to earth and begin looking for another animal. This time it is an elephant. It is quite far, on the left side of matatu. It is a young male, eating leaves from a nearest bush. It stops for a while and looks at the vehicle. The driver stops the car so that it is more convenient to take pictures.

The elephant like in a tacit cooperation begins to come closer. I am happy to get better and better shots every few seconds with the object of my admiration coming closer and closer, I cannot stop taking pictures. Moving its head left and right, and lifting and twisting its trunk around its tusks, the elephant begins to move faster and faster toward me.

Still not realizing the danger and increasing speed of the animal, I keep on taking pictures. Among the sound of the flash of my camera, I hear the driver saying that we should go. It is like I am in a trance waiting until the last moment, for the elephant to come closer still. Finally I shout "go."

The matatu pulls away, followed by the heavy animal. Initially, the distance is still getting closer and closer, the vehicle I am in does not seem

reliable enough to escape this creature. I am scared, but soon the arrow on the speedometer begins to rise, and the elephant is left behind, still waiving the trunk warning us not to bother it anymore. As soon as I find myself at a safe distance, I start to laugh. It is quite an exciting story to tell.

After about two more hours of driving, I arrive at one of the exclusive lodges in the Maasai Mara Game Park. Nice and welcoming entrance to the lodge, attracts tourists not only to relax outside on the terrace or near the fancy swimming pool but stay here for longer in the comfortable apartments, and buy overly priced souvenirs in their store. I rest for a little over 30 minutes and leave the place to continue my safari trip.

Topi, gazelle, impala, and a couple more giraffes.

All of them are roaming in different directions, crossing unwritten boundaries drawn through the savanna by men or predators. Maasai Mara is big. I have already seen a lot of herbivores. Muscular and smooth, some standing, some lying down, some eating or fighting, but always in a crowd.

A crowd is safer than alone. In a land where everything alive has to watch out every second or it may lose its life, a crowd is the best security system.

Each crowd is armed with few stronger members being on the outside, watching for danger, ready to warn the rest and run. Run for their lives. But sometimes, one in the crowd is weaker, or just unlucky, and stays behind. Too slow, and does not manage to escape the wild hunter, not surviving. But this weaker ones sacrifice saves the whole herd. That counts.

Contrasting with the herbivores, a few kilometers away almost on the track that could be called road, I see a few lionesses. Cuddling with each other, they fall into a deep sleep. I am so close that I can almost touch them.

So dangerous, but so cute.

Looking at them sleeping, seeing them breathing as their chests move up and down, covered with yellowish or straw like color fur, I think that they look deceptively harmless.

I take several pictures. The lionesses do not seem to be bothered by my presence there at all. The driver then explains why the lion is considered to be the king of animals. This belief is shared by numerous cultures and populations even outside Africa. It has its base in the fact that the lion is the only animal that is not afraid of any other creature, being self-

91

To Be... in Africa

aware of its power, proudly carrying itself, feeling the respect that others give to him.

And the confirmation is right in front of me. Several lionesses sleeping less than fifty centimeters away, not bothered by the flash of my camera. They know I am not a threat to them, and that is true.

As I drive away I look ahead. Far, far in front of me, I see hills, I try to catch some stable point, something I can rest my eyes on, something very far, as far as I can see it. But the horizon seems endless. I look on the sides. All the same.

Surrounded by hills, which are surrounded by hills, and those also surrounded by hills. All those hills, huge hills, increase the area of the park. Maasai Mara is so big. Kenya is so big. Transfixed by the expanse of it all I feel so small, so harmless, so vulnerable. But then I also feel empowered by being there by having the chance to experience the limit, to go where not everyone goes, to see the border of reality and eternity.

Finally, it is about mid afternoon, and time to eat. The matatu stops nearby the Tanzania border. Before the driver prepares the sandwiches, and takes the drinks out, I wander away with one of the guards to the neighboring country. He led me on a

narrow path to a river. I come as close to the edge as I can, spotting few hippopotamuses cooling down in the water. One of them comes out and is followed by a young one. A beautiful view, and also a great river. Very wide. It sculpted the architecture of this area for many years, shaping tall cliffs that surround it. I take several pictures and return for my meal.

I roam around the park for a little more and start heading back. It is getting dark when I arrive at the camp. I can feel my muscles hurt like after some heavy workout. Even though I spent almost all the time inside the matatu, I feel tired. Numerous bumps and ditches are tough to handle. I lie on my bed in the tent. I feel the temperature dropping down. It gets chilly again.

I decide to get up and check if dinner is ready. It is - chapatis, rice, stew, vegetables...and inseparable chai. I warm myself up. And after dinner, still wanting to stay like that, I commit my time to sitting close to the bonfire. It gets dark around. Only the light from the fire allows me to see who is sitting next to me. The heat is almost burning, but I do not want to move away. I stay here, like I am glued to the place. I am looking at the fire. My mind starts to wander away again. That seems to happen very often lately.

Again, I think about where I am. I think what I have seen and have gone through. The story of my young life pops in front of my mind's eye. There are so many things I want to share, so many memories.

So young…and still so many more to come.

With an abrupt return to reality, I look around. I cannot see much, but what I see is unique itself. The fire is in front of me, a yellow flame with a halo around it - something majestic! I look higher.

The sky.

Beautiful, black sky illuminated with thousands of stars. They seem to be closer here than anywhere else… multiple stars and constellations. The moon, it looks like a big sickle with both ends pointing upward. It reminds me of a little baby's cradle; cradle of humanity maybe?

Kenya is a most natural and primeval place; a place where basic instincts arise. As if to confirm my thoughts, I see behind me a Maasai warrior. He stands there with his long spear. Almost still, he looks upon the fire with a kind of respect and subordination to this power. Silent. Beautiful in his timeless form; traditional, original, true.

It is unique to be in Kenya, to sit next to the fire, at night. Fire that burns and brings something new. And hearing sounds of the savanna night with the silent guards who, like ghosts, are there but do not look real. That somehow makes me feel safe, safe and relaxed. Safe and convinced that this is a place where I belong, where everything starts.

A place where I feel one with nature.

The kingdom of timeless elements.

May 23, 2007

I'm shivering, again. It's cold outside, but the temperature inside the tent does not differ much. 6:30 Am. I have to get up. It's still dark and with my only half-open eyes I barely find my way to the matatu. I load my baggage and go to eat. Soon I am leaving this place to head back to Nairobi. Three young Maasai are helping to load the cars. I decide to ask them if I can take a picture with them. I have been told Maasai do not usually allow for that. Seeing tourists with cameras pointed at them, they explicitly communicate not to take pictures. I can understand that being a part of a living culture and encountering multiple tourists, who want to take picture of them and their family to have a souvenir

To Be... in Africa

from the trip to Kenya, can be annoying and sometimes also offensive. Therefore, a little anxious of the reaction of the two Maasai men standing nearby, I approach them and politely ask if I can have a picture with them.

They agree.

Perhaps it is because I stayed in Maasai Mara and interacted with them for the last three days. They already know me, or maybe it is the moments we shared around bonfire bonding time when we just sat silently nearby each other looking at the little particles of fire shooting high into the darkness of the night.

Finally all is loaded. The sun begins to rise. The driver leads the car slowly between hills. The surroundings begin to change gradually. It gets more tight with fewer open spaces, more trees and bushes, and something that resembles a road more and more.

In a few hours, I reach the city of Narok. Grabbing the bags that I left there on the way to the Game Park, I am on the way to Nairobi. The travel back is not as rough as some others I had have. The driver is speeding and the only thing that seems to stop him from going twice as fast as the legal speed limit, are the holes on the road. Passing through the dusty towns where millions of red clay particles are stirring the air making me unable to see far ahead, I am falling asleep.

Finally, I arrive in Nairobi. Getting back to the house I stayed at in the beginning is good. I have dinner and get ready to sleep.

May 24, 2007

I stretch my body on the bed. It feels good. I open my eyes and look at the clock curiously. It is 8:37am. I slept for over nine hours, feeling as fresh as the morning outside my window, rested and full of energy to conquer another day. I get dressed and go downstairs, following the smell of freshly made breakfast.

The day seems to go smoothly, spontaneously, not planned at all. Around noon, I go to Adam's Arcade, a nearby shopping center where I can get a good lunch and use the internet. I stay there until dinner time, which I have in the same restaurant. Minutes are passing by slowly. I have no idea of what I should do today. I just sit among big banana trees and enjoy being in Kenya. I observe people doing their routines, tourists walking somewhere close to me, I listen to the noise made by cars driving on the street only a few yards from me. I like it. For a break from sitting, I go to a few stores to get some nice postcards that I can send out the next day to my family and friends.

I check my e-mail, reply to some messages that I received during the past few days, read the news, and go back to my resting place that I occupied almost all day.

The day goes by; it seems like I did not do anything special or exciting, same place to eat, same store to visit, same seat that I used all day long. But actually that's just an illusion. I think I need to slow down. I need to be like Kenyans for a moment, not worrying about doing something all the time, being in a hurry, working, walking, almost running through life.

So I just sit down.

I have no plans for today. I just rest. I look at myself and at others. This is something you cannot do when rushing in life. I look back on the days that I have spent here. I look even farther back, as far as I can remember. I think about my life, about my experiences, about my plans and hopes for the future. My mind is busy from thoughts crossing it in every direction. But I need that. I need to just sit and think. Think about me being in Kenya and what it means to me, how it affects me.

I am still, looking somewhere, at another invisible point hanging very far away, behind the building, behind the fence, behind imagination. My eyes are not really looking at the surroundings anymore. It is just me. The pictures are changing around faster and faster, and I am slowing down. It seems like my time flows differently than theirs. It looks like I am watching a movie while someone pushed the "fast forward" button.

Then it stops.

I look around me. People are busy with their business and nobody even knows how my universe has transformed. I give someone a weird look, surprised how he can be so indifferent to what I went through. But he does not know. Nobody knows. It is just my escape, escape into the world of philosophy, world of seeking to find the answers, world where if you are careful enough, you realize that the answer is not important, but the seeking itself.

The rest of the day goes by in the usual rhythm: dinner, meeting with the group concerning planning for the next few days, walk back to the house, spending some time with my friends, and finally sleep. Someone would say it is a boring day, well, it is not very eventful, that is true, but nobody can say it was a wasted day. A day when you come to realize something new, a day when you learn something new is never a wasted day.

May 25, 2007

I wake up, take a shower and get dressed. The house is quiet. I go down the stairs to the kitchen where I find breakfast ready: egg and sausages, mandazis and chai. I eat it in silence, enjoying the smell of the food spreading in the air. Today I am going to visit one of the most famous orphanages in Kenya - Thomas Barnardo Orphanage.

I arrive at the gate. Two guards ask me about the purpose of my visit and let me in. The area for the orphanage is big, covered with buildings designed for different purposes: cafeterias, classes, dorms for girls, dorms for boys, newborns, children in kindergarten, elementary school and high school. The orphanage produces its own bread and manufactures several other items with the help of the older kids. Girls are trained to make clothes, while boys get experience in more physical activities. There are about three hundred kids who find a home in the Thomas Barnardo Orphanage.

I do not get to see many of the kids, since it is Friday, and many of them are in school. The only place I can go to meet the children is the nursery. The lady who is giving the tour explains the process of adoption and tells several stories of how some of them have ended up in that orphanage. Sadly, there is a huge number of newborns rejected by their mothers. The majority of them find peace here, while some are left in hospitals, some are abandoned in the garbage for certain death.

One of the little girls that I spot and take into my arms has a similar story. Born as a pre-mature baby, she was left on the dumpster wrapped in some fabrics to die in a cruel way. Luckily, someone noticed her tiny body moving and brought her to the gate of this orphanage, where she was taken care of. Her critical condition, being malnourished, and exhausted, soon began to improve. Now, she is a couple of months old, and even though she is still very tiny and weak like a persistent memory of what she went through, she is one of the babies that catches the most attention.

Daria Barwinska

So touching.

The life of these little innocent, abandoned children is already full of sad stories.

So young to know cruelty and abandonment.

So young to know hardship.

It is uplifting to know that there are people who care for the fate of these kids and want to make their life happier, putting a smile on their faces. How precious is a smile on a child's face!

(A few weeks later, after leaving Kenya, I received a Thank you note from the orphanage – it can be viewed in the Appendix section of this book.)

On the way back from the orphanage, penetrating the rough streets full of cars and skillful drivers who to me seem to take too much risk, I stop by a Post Office to mail a couple of postcards to my family and friends. All of them have a nice picture of animals with a little saying "Greetings from Kenya." On every one, I write in Post Scriptum the cliché "I wish you were here" because no words or pictures would help me to describe Kenya and what I have experienced here.

In the afternoon, I am taken by my Kenyan friends for a tour around Nairobi. I pass by their old schools they used to go to. I pass by a beautiful Hindu temple. I pass by a series of hotels and stores. Silent, I look through the window of the car. Images are changing instantly from houses to a wall of trees, from city traffic and cars that are as close as it is possible, to empty back roads divided with tall fences. Some remind me of home, some are very contrasting.

Wealth and poverty.

People walking somewhere to a destination known only to them. They walk slowly, not in a hurry. Kenyans have this unique attitude to enjoy every minute and not to rush life. They are chilled, living their lives like in a slow motion picture. It is an odd look and a fascinating one at the same time.

Finally, I reach Village Market, which, contrary to the name, is not just a "village" market. With widely opened eyes, I become stunned by a breathtaking upscale shopping center. Numerous buildings are connected to each other by a complex of bridges creating a circle. I enter the mall, climbing the stairs to the first floor. Passing between stores, I find myself on the opposite site to where I entered, facing this time not the outside with the car park, but the inside with a little artificial lake, waterfall, places to rest and food court. It is a stunning place. Very modern and elegant. I enter a few stores, Gucci, Dior, a souvenir store, all of them very expensive. I walk for a little while, getting inspired by the view. My attention is grabbed by a little store selling decorations made with stained glass. Some of them are exhibited outside, being a part of the architecture of the store itself. What a wonderful picture. The sunrays entering the center of this mall shine directly on the colorful glass surface, reflecting from it millions of colors projecting in every direction. The closeness of water makes the atmosphere even more magical.

Finally, I turn back and go to the top level. Usually it is a car park, but today it is transformed into a crowded event called Maasai market where anyone could get anything to commemorate a trip to East Africa. I wander around, trying to find my way between people who are buying and those who are selling. Trying not to step onto any of the items displayed on the ground, I do not know where to look. There are loads of jewelry, traditional dresses, wooden carvings, cases and bowls made of soapstone, boutiques. Everything that one could think of is here to buy.

I am distracted. I try to concentrate. I want to see all the items and talk to all the sellers, but it is impossible. There are too many of them. In this chaos of shopping for souvenirs, something I have not really done yet, I try to figure out what I should get for my family and friends and for myself. It is not the easiest thing to do. I want to get some figures of animals carved in wood, batiks, some soapstone boxes, and some other items. All that I would like to have is here. One of them is a Maasai shield and two spears. As I walk around with my friend, I spot one exactly the size and shape that I want. Now the real challenge is to come - bargaining with the seller for the final price I am going to pay.

The starting prices that many Kenyans are giving to white, tourist-looking people can be even as much as twenty times as high as the "real" value of the product. Some people pay that much, but I decide to barter. Usually, tourists are not able to get items as cheap as locals would. My friend Emily is with me. She, knowing how much I want the shield, does all the bargaining and manages to get as low a price as possible. In the stream of words in Kiswahili, I hear some that meant "friend" and "white person" which is described by the word mzungu. But that is the only part of the whole long conversation that I can understand. Standing a little on the side, I am trying to catch a glimpse of some other items that I can possibly get, but ultimately all my concentration is directed to the outcome of the bargain between my friend and the seller. Finally, the price is set, and I like it. I get my shield and two spears, which makes my day. Dizzy with happiness from the last purchase, even though not carried out by me directly, I get even more distracted and unable to make any more logical decisions about the souvenirs I want to buy. I wander a little more, see a little more of what is displayed and decide to leave since the rest of the time would be unproductive anyway.

In the evening, after supper, I relax, sitting in a comfortable armchair. I think about the past few days, realizing more and more that the time for me to leave Kenya is coming soon. I do not want to leave yet, but then I also know that when I leave, I will be equipped with experiences and memories.

May 26, 2007

I wake up later than usual. It's going to be a day of shopping for souvenirs - one of the banally exciting parts of every travel. Fun on one hand, and sometimes annoying on the other when I'm not sure what to get. Even as I start the day, I do not know what I should get for my family and friends. I try to match the items with the architecture of their houses, hobbies, or personalities, and even though it is a good idea to start with, it does not make it any easier. I still have a lot of doubts, bombarded by sudden ideas, which as soon as they come, they are disintegrating under the influence of emerging counterarguments, producing reason good enough to overthrow my theory. For a balance to the intense race of thoughts about gifts, my mind goes blank. I do not have even the slightest idea what I should buy and for how many people.

In this mixture of semi-philosophical, semi-practical devotions I run downstairs to grab some mandazis and enter the taxi that takes me to the Maasai market. I am with my Kenyan friends. I hold on to them as I enter a crowded square covered with booths where people are selling their merchandise.

With my purse as close to me as possible, I try to find my way among the carpets of soapstone bowls, chess-sets, wooden figures, jewelry, and more importantly the sellers. The appearance of a white person who must almost certainly be a tourist seems to alert all of them. Like bees flying to honey, they shout from every direction encouraging me to visit their place. Some are just asking me to stop by and take a look, some go far beyond that, pointing at particular items they have and asking me to buy it. As if they magically know what I need. They call: "buy the candle holder, look how nice it is. You won't find it anywhere else." "This is unique, the material is unique, and the carving is of the best quality," they add, surprisingly blindly believing or hoping that I cannot see the exact items displayed by numerous other salesmen around me. Many of them go even farther by physically blocking my way or pulling or pushing me toward their little booths and displays.

I hear many times that the items they have displayed are the only genuine ones, and that they make them themselves. However, the truth very often lies in between. For an inexperienced tourist, a wooden carving painted black, can look like a ebony carving, which is of higher quality. Very often, the items displayed are not made by the people who sell them. They buy them from the real manufacturers for a ridiculously and sadly cheap price, exploiting their work and time, and sell it for even twenty times as much, getting a high profit. However, some Kenyans, whom I met at the market, are genuine artists working constantly on new carvings or jewelry while I am trying to decide what to get from their little booth. Some are honest enough to admit what material something is made of, at the same time suggesting a very reasonable price. It requires skill. Shopping and bartering at the Maasai market is not easy. Spending a lot of money for something that is not what it is supposed to be is not uncommon.

In the craze of people rushing to sell me things, adding that they have a special discount (often using their imagination to the furthest extent to come up with some reasonably sounding explanations, which seem very forced), I slowly collect more and more items that I like and want to take home with me.

Among countless items, I also begin to find those that I consider a good gift for my family and friends, based on some unexplainable presumptions that this is what they would like the most.

Three o'clock. I decide to leave the crowded place. I feel like I have enough souvenirs. Besides that, the bargaining, although it can be fun, after the whole day of practicing, it gets tiring and without a fresh mind, it gets harder and harder to make good decisions connected with purchasing certain items.

I expect this evening to be eventful. A quarter to six and I am getting ready for dinner with the Ananis, a couple that runs the Frepals Clinic in Kibera. I put on the most formal clothes I have with me. Soon I am in a car on my way to the restaurant, where the Ananis are to meet us. It is already dark, according to the old tradition of nature. As I arrive at the place, I am quite amused by the architecture. Our seats were outside, which was a good idea, considering the refreshing wind of the evening, and sounds and smells that are floating in the air.

The Ananis are already here. We all place our orders and begin talking about the experiences in Africa. We jump from time to time to more random conversations involving food, sport, politics, and some daily events. It is a good time. Among the laughter, we all make stronger bonds with each other. Smiling eyes of everyone at the table say that we all enjoy ourselves so much, and want to preserve this time as long as possible.

This wonderful moment lasts until an even more moving and unspeakable event takes place. Freda and Paul Anani hand gifts to these few of us who got to go to their Clinic a few days ago.

It is so unexpected, not because it would be hard to believe to get a gift from these two wonderful and devoted people, but unexpected to get a gift from people who do not appear to have anything themselves, yet they still give to others. These are wonderful gifts with our names engraved in the items they got us.

Individual gifts.

So much more precious because we received them from someone full of humbleness and love.

So moving.

To Be... in Africa

So difficult to describe.

Another wonderful experience of true thanks and gratitude.

Tears of joy and emotion mix with smiles and light faces. A moment of silence is broken by thousands of "Thank You" words, words of admiration, words of appreciation, but still not enough to fully express the feelings. A mountain of words would not be enough. But they know how much we are touched. They feel it. They see it in our eyes, watering eyes, shining in the darkness of the evening from the joy and unspeakable feelings. A drop from my eye slowly marks the gift wrap. The air is charged with emotion.

Both Freda and Paul are smiling, watching us surprised. They look happy. There is something very calm in them, something that is so respectful about them. Their faces show that they have been through a lot of hardship in their lives, but they learned to enjoy life and every small moment of happiness that it brings. Their faces are full of wisdom that just by looking at them I feel detached from the common reality. I feel uplifted and fulfilled.

Tonight I promise myself I will not stop here. I promise this trip to Kenya is only the beginning of something greater. I will carry on the support for Africa, and I will carry on the dedication for giving a better life to those in need.

A few minutes later, a waiter brings our food. It is delicious. Biting off big parts of goat meat, I dive into discussion about Kenyan cuisine. I should also add that since I have never had goat meat before, this is quite a new experience. I cannot really compare the taste to anything else that I know of, but it definitely has a different texture. Smoked meat tastes very good, even though a little bit harder than pork or beef, it has a unique taste that I have never encountered before.

The rest of the night goes well, among laughs and talks we all enjoy ourselves.

May 27, 2007

Sunday morning. Time to get up and get ready for church. It is my last visit to church in Kenya during this trip. I almost get there late. The big building glitters with its whiteness from far away. In front at the main gate, there is a crowd of people who gathered after the first service at nine in the morning. I decide to mingle for a bit and meet new people, finally entering the church. It is very spacious. Long, rectangular lamps are hanging from the enormous ceiling. The altar, decorated nicely, is elevated above the floor so that everyone can see the speaker. This church must have been designed for a larger amount of people, the countless rows of seats seem to point the way for the followers who come to have their part in the spiritual devotion. It really is a big building, lightened by a few lamps and sunrays entering the place through small windows with stained-glass.

The service though is not very special. One speaker seems to get a bit over emotional and excited about the topic she is speaking of. It borders with some false exaltations. I don't like that. There is no humbleness.

Later on, I have lunch, a sandwich with fresh vegetables. I also go to Nakumat - the department store in Nairobi where I used to go every so often to get food. This time I go there again, hoping I can spot some interesting item that I did not see before. Walking from store to store, realizing that these are my last few days of this trip, I try to absorb as many of the images that pass before my eyes as I can.

I spend more time in the stores, talking to the salesmen, enjoying every bit of my interactions with them and getting invigorated by Kiswahili bytes flowing around my ears.

I walk back to the house and start packing. It is not an easy task either. Coming here I already had a full suitcase, and now, leaving this beautiful country, I have even more items, including souvenirs or findings, it seems impossible to pack everything into one small container. I decide to leave a few things: clothes, towels, shoes. The space I gain is soon filled with the things I bought here.

I pack and repack thousands of times, trying new arrangements, new ways of folding, but reality is screaming: one suitcase is not enough. Finally I manage to close my bag.

Afternoon is passing by slowly. To make it more productive, I go for a ride around the city; last one during this trip. I sit still on the back seat of the car of one of my Kenyan friends, looking at the scenes passing by my window. I must have said that before: driving in Kenya is challenging. Grasping a few more memories from the streets of Nairobi, I watch my friends driving, and the situation in front of the car. In Kenya, people drive on the left side of the road, a reminder of the earlier colonial influences of the British Empire. Somehow that does not seem right to me, being used to right sides, and in combination with the lack of street lights, the traffic makes me nervous. Cars are everywhere, almost touching each other. On one street line, designed for one line of cars, there are three lines of cars, some almost entering sidewalks. And people walking in between them, crossing the street. It is chaotic. But everything in that chaos is ordered. It

looks like a big anthill...like one body pulsating, living.

When I am turning away my attention from the roads to the sides, I see the city of Nairobi. Schools, stores, embassies, beautiful and majestic Hindu temple above the horizon, and many more. Finally, still in the car, and still driving around, I close my eyes, as if they are too tired to absorb any more of these images. I find myself sitting, just sitting there, knowing I should look outside, listen to the noise, but that's not what I do. I feel tired like the darkness behind my eyelids is soothing and necessary at that moment. All the noises seem to flow away from me. I stay like that for a while, recharging my batteries, thinking, resting. When I open my eyes, we are still driving, driving past the wall of trees, houses, familiar streets, and finally through the gate to the house where I am staying.

Dinner is different than usual. No chapatis, no ugali, and no chai. Sitting in the Kenyan scenery, having a view of palm-looking short trees, and hearing noises of some night birds, I eat a delicious pizza with pineapple, sipping Coke from a glass bottle. Taking my time. And thinking. Again. Too much for today.

May 28, 2007

Even though my suitcase was ready the previous day, standing at the door, waiting to be put into the trunk of a car, I decide I need to take a final look inside. I open it, having this odd hope that I can still rearrange things, but rationality is telling me not to touch anything anymore because I will spend the next few hours trying to put it back in as effective way as it is all ordered now. I lock it and take it down the stairs to the front door.

Day just goes by fast and it is dinner time. Last dinner before I leave the family that has so wonderfully hosted me in Kenya, and with my dear friend Emily, the one who just simply told me to go home with her in May.

So priceless. And here I leave. A lot of hugs, a lot of good words, a lot of tears that are making their way to the corners of my eyes. It takes some time. Finally, someone says I need to hurry, I have just a little bit over an hour and a half to get to the airport, go through security check-in and board the plane. Driving to the airport is done in a hurry. I am almost late, as continuing the Kenyan tradition. Looking through the window, I catch a last glimpse of the illuminated city of Nairobi at night.

The craze at the airport is unbelievable. Right before entering the building, I receive and give away a few more hugs of farewell.

Moving and sad.

I check-in, hoping that my bag is not over the weight limit. To my surprise, it is not. Finally, I board the plane. I find my seat and make myself comfortable. In a few more minutes, the plane begins to take off, and I am in the air again, on my way back home. I see the dark night through the window; it looks the same as the one I saw when I arrived here three weeks ago. I close my eyes. Thoughts are running through my head. But finally, I fall into a deep sleep.

A deserved sleep, with dreams of Kenya.

May 29, 2007

Familiar looking land beneath me. Feels like déjà vu. London again. I arrive on time. Exit, checkpoint, bag search. All done quite fast. Too fast, as now I have over five hours of waiting to board the plane to Chicago. I go for a walk inside the terminal, Channel, Gucci, D&G. The stores attract. Later I sit down on the bench, eat my crackers that I bought the day before in Nairobi. The same ones that because of which my bag was searched. I am not tired, but I try to sleep. In between these short naps, I watch people passing by. Time seems like it is not passing by at all. Finally, after a couple of hours that seem like an eternity, I board the plane to the United States. I am taking off. Yes, I am coming back. In a few hours, I will see my friends again. Sitting in the middle section I cannot see a lot of what is outside the window, but flying over the ocean does not provide a very exciting view either. I fall asleep. I sleep all the way to Chicago, waking up only to get a meal served by an overly nice plane crew, repeating the same phrase over and over to every passenger: "chicken or beef?" Some kind of feeling sorry for this situation crosses my mind. But it disappears as fast as it comes when I get my food.

Here I am again. Chicago O'Hare airport. Now, 4 hour drive home. But that does not matter anymore. I am back. I am on the ground.

Finally Anderson, Indiana. Parking lot.

The same place where the whole journey began. I am back. Great feeling. But not the only one. It's mixed with some emotion of fulfillment, wisdom and spiritual richness, but also of missing those days that passed and all those things that I didn't get to see and learn.

I am back and the trip is over, but it is not the end.

It's just the beginning.

Beginning of a longer story, greater in size and power...

APPENDIX

17th July 2007

Dear Friend,

RE : THANK YOU

We acknowledge receipt of your recent donation to our Home.

Thomas Barnardo House seeks to restore, maintain and educate orphaned, abandoned or destitute children ranging from newborn babies in the nursery to early twenties in the transition cases. We are wholly reliant on donations and well wishers. Your donation of clothes & shoes went along way in assisting us meet the needs of our 178 children.

Without your friendship and others like you, we would not be able to carry on.

So again, on behalf of the children and the Barnardo fraternity, please accept our sincere thanks.

Yours sincerely,

A. Kiraithe

CHIEF ADMINISTRATOR

CONCLUSION

When the heat, of the events, cool down like a log in a fireplace that someone extinguished. When you can't forget all the injustices you have seen. Do you allow yourself to give in and surrender to indifference in a forceless anger? Are you like a cold rock like a monument of pride and unresponsiveness?

Knowing, and doing nothing with it, is a wasted opportunity.

I have seen beautiful things and I have seen sorrowful things. I have learned, and I don't want to leave it behind. Too many tears of joy and sadness went down my face.

I realize that fractions people's stories, reality, the world, reach our eyes and ears. But you can learn more...

If you never push yourself to seek the truth, reality, the limits, your limits, you won't ever know yourself, and you won't live a full life of understanding the world and your role in it.

That is the road to take: a road to redemption, a road to knowledge of who you are and what you do.

I have drawn a story...

A real story that I experienced and that impacted me.

I have drawn a story of rhythm.

A story of a country whose heart beats to the sound of the African drums.

I have drawn a story of freeing a body and mind.

I have drawn a story.

I used words, but there are none that can really show the image that I have in my heart.

conclusion

PHOTO ALBUM

My good friend Emily stands in the middle with one of her friends from home. This is in Frepals Clinic and they are talking to the amazing Freda Anani. Kibera Slum (below)

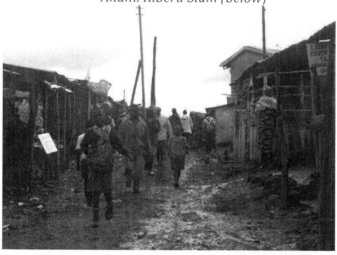

Friends from my trip with kids at church, our first Sunday

KHBC dorm room with the mosquito net.

Girls from our group with our friends at KHBC.

This is the professor from KHBC who I encountered in Kericho town after my experience in the dump.

Lion with Buffalo in Mara

Me on safari

conclusion

Maasai church leader in Transmara where leaders are intentional about celebrating their traditional cultural. (Photo by SR Martin)

This is me celebrating standing at the Kenya Tanzania boarder in Maasai Mara.

Accepting a gift from the Ananis

Kima, or Vervet Monkey –I experienced in both Kericho and Maasai Mara.

Accepting gift from Freda Anani

At orphanage

3135483

Made in the USA